Inviting Jesus Into Your Heart
Understanding your new life as a born-again Believer

Wordflowers

Misha G. Benjamin

Unless otherwise noted, all scripture is taken from the New King James Version of The Holy Bible.

"Scripture taken from the New King James Version Copyright 1982 by Thomas Nelson, Inc Used by permission. All rights reserved."

"Scripture quoted from The Holy Bible, New Century Version, copyright 1987, 1988, 1991 by Word Publishing, a division of Thomas Nelson, Inc Used by permission."

"Scripture quotations taken from AMPLIFIED BIBLE, Copyright ©1954, 1958, 1962, 1964, 1965, 1987 by The Lockman Foundation. All rights reserved. Used by permission (www.Lockman.org)."

Inviting Jesus Into Your Heart
ISBN-10: 0988640309
ISBN-13: 978-0-9886403-0-6

Published by The Wordflowers Corporation
©Inviting Jesus into your Heart
2013 Wordflowers®

Your questions, inquiries, and requests for more information are welcome at: info@wordflowerscorp.org. You may also visit our website at www.wordflowerscorp.org. You may also contact us by mail at:

Wordflowers
Post Office Box 406
Occoquan, Virginia 22125

Library of Congress Control Number: 2013931822

Printed and distributed in the United States of America and Internationally. All rights reserved under International Copyright Law. No part of this book may be reproduced or transmitted in any form or by any means, electronic or mechanical, including photocopying, recording, or by any information storage and retrieval system, without the written permission of the publisher.

Dedication

I dedicate this book to my Wonderful Mother, Ms. Alberta Benjamin. Mom, I dedicate this book to you because you trained me in the ways that I should go. I have learned that the true end and scope of life is God. Mom, I thank you for introducing me to Jesus and taking me to church and to places where I learned about life and about Jesus at an early age. Thank you for giving me my first Bible when I was very young. I really loved reading it as a child and I still enjoy reading, hearing, and listening to God's Word. Thank you for teaching me to pray and to be obedient to the Word of God. I am Thankful to God and my Lord and Savior Jesus Christ!

And I am thankful for you, Mom.

Table of Contents

Introduction: Inviting Jesus into your Heart ..*13*

Chapter One **1** : *The Medicine for Sin* *17*

Chapter Two **2** : *Walking in Love through Dangers Unseen* *23*

Chapter Three **3** : *Be Strong! Be Brave on your Journey!* *29*

Chapter Four **4** : *For you, your Nation, and all accompanying you* *37*

Chapter Five **5** : *Spiritual and Eternal Salvation Now!* *43*

Table of Contents continued........

Prayer and Baptism in the Holy Spirit 49

You are more than a Conqueror!......................51

About Jesus 53

About the Author...59

Upcoming Book Releases!..................................61

For more information about Wordflowers......63

Notes 65

INTRODUCTION

INVITING JESUS INTO YOUR HEART

"Come to Me, all you who labor and are heavy laden, and I will give you rest. Take My yoke upon you and learn from Me, for I am gentle and lowly in heart, and you will find rest for your souls. For My yoke is easy and My burden is light."
Matthew 11:28-30

Our Living Word, the Gospel of Jesus Christ, is the power of God to salvation for everyone who believes (Rom.1:16). Believing God and inviting Jesus into your heart is the most important part of living victorious in this life. Inviting Jesus into your heart and confessing that He is Lord brings all the benefits of salvation into your life, more than you could ever expect, exceedingly abundantly above all you could ever ask or think (Ephesians 3:20). Your salvation (*solteria*) in Christ speaks of the present experiences of God's power to deliver and preserve you from the bondage of sin (Matt. 1:21; Rom. 5:10; Heb. 7:25; James 1:21; 1 Cor. 15:2).

Sin causes trouble and suffering to be inflicted upon the sinner but Jesus has come to be your great Deliverer and Redeemer. Sin may also refer to the trouble and suffering that one may inflict upon others. There is nothing too difficult for God to Deliver you out of. Living a life of sin is simply the wrong path for anyone to take and to continue to journey on; it is a twisting out of the right way of life that God wants you to live. God has a great path of abundant life and victory for you to live (John 10:10). In this life, God will bountifully equip you with all that you need to come out victoriously.

In this book I will discuss and answer questions such as: What can I do to remove and forgive sin?; What does it mean to walk in love?; What are the many benefits of salvation and what does it mean for me and my life?; and Why is it important to Believe in Jesus?

Chapter One

THE MEDICINE FOR SIN

"In Him we have redemption through His blood, the forgiveness of sins, according to the riches of His grace." Ephesians 1:7

There is only one cure for the sin in our lives and it is the Blood of Jesus. By the Grace of God, The Lord gave us His Son Jesus Christ to remove and forgive our sins and wrongdoings forever. When Jesus died and was resurrected His blood became remitting blood that will forever wash and remove all of our sins both past, present, and future just as if nothing never happened. God now sees you and me as He sees His Son Jesus.

When Jesus was resurrected, His new life was then given to us. Now, we are DAILY delivered from the bondages of sin through His resurrection life (Romans 5:10 AMP).

In this new resurrection life, you must take the Blood of Jesus like medicine and apply it to every situation and circumstance in your life. You do this by having faith in what His Blood has accomplished. When you begin your new life with Jesus you will learn to fear the Lord by departing away from every evil.

And to man He said, 'Behold, the fear of the Lord, that is wisdom, And to depart from evil is understanding'(Job 28:28).

We are to get this understanding if it costs us everything we've got. (Proverbs 4:1-7; Job 28:28). To depart from evil means that you have left your past life and your previous path of sin and you have taken God's path designed especially for you in your life. You can take this path that God has for you by daily renewing your mind in God's Word. Doing this will help you to take off your former conduct called, 'the old man', and put on your new way of life called, 'the new man':

> ....*and that you put on the new man which was created according to God, in true righteousness and holiness (Ephesians 4:24).*

All of the suffering trouble, evil, guilt, sorrow, falsehood, deception, and wickedness is washed away and forgiven forever. You have become washed and cleansed in the Blood of Jesus! You are now a new creature in Christ Jesus (2 Cor. 5:17).

This new life also presents to you many newfound salvation benefits of victory and triumph. The vastly manifold benefits of salvation include: material and temporal deliverance from danger and apprehension; National and personal deliverance, spiritual and eternal deliverance; and also the promise of the Holy Spirit, which is the guarantee of your inheritance

(Eph. 1:13-14).

The Holy Spirit is your leader, teacher and guide. Once you trust and have faith in the Holy Spirit, He will be with you forever. God will give you insight regarding the Holy Spirit. The Holy Spirit of God loves you and will always be there for you. When you surrender yourself to the Holy Spirit, you will never be alone again.

The Holy Spirit will save you and transform you into the person that God has ordained you to be. The Spirit of God is the Name of The Holy Spirit that is associated with power, prophecy and guidance. It is the Holy Spirit that covers our guilt with His righteousness through faith when we believe. The Holy Spirit will keep His promise and will rest on you. You only need to trust in Him. (1 Sam. 10:10; Ezek. 11:24-25).

Chapter Two

WALKING IN LOVE THROUGH DANGERS UNSEEN

"And walk in love, [esteeming and delighting in one another] as Christ loved us and gave Himself up for us, a slain offering and sacrifice to God [for you, so that it became] a sweet fragrance." [Ezek. 20:41.] (Eph. 5:2) Amp.

God sent Jesus His Son to be your salvation and that includes material and temporal deliverance from danger and apprehension. Being in danger is being faced with any risk that binds, makes guilty, insecure, dangerous, or prone to fall. Jesus never wants you to fear anything or anyone. He says over and over again in His Word that we are to FEAR NOT (Matt. 10:31; Luke 12:32; John 12:15). Your salvation in Jesus triumphs over every fear, danger, and difficulty in this life:

> *[God] disarmed the principalities and powers that were ranged against us and made a bold display and public example of them, in triumphing over them in Him and in it [the cross] (Col. 2:15 Amp.).*

By boldly approaching the throne of grace you welcome Him into every room of your life at every moment of your life (Heb.4:16). Where His presence is there is no fear or danger, only love (1 John 4:8-10, 18). That is why it is important to walk in love.

Have you ever wondered what it means to walk in love? I have found that walking in love is closely connected to humility. The Word of God teaches plainly all the ways we are to walk in love and humility. The Word of God gives Jesus as our great example. Jesus always has our best interest in His heart. Jesus is our great High Priest and Intercessor. He is interceding on our behalf both day and night before the Father (Hebrews 7:25-27).

In 2 Chronicles 7:14 God forewarns Israel to humble themselves by prayer, seeking God's face, and repentance. To repent is to turn from wicked ways and go in a new, healthy and better direction. I must tell you that the ways of God is the best direction to walk in. When these actions are taken, God promises that He will hear from Heaven, and will forgive your sin and heal your land. There are also many New Testament examples, such as Philippians 2:3 where the Apostle Paul mentions the practice of edifying (building) and encouraging others while viewing them as more important than yourself (Phil. 2:3; Col. 3:12; 1 Pet. 5:5). This is the individual action of Believers toward each other (1 Cor. 8:1;10:23; 1 Thess. 5:11).

    Jesus gave us this principle to help us to comprehend with all the saints what is the width and length and depth and height to know the love of Christ which passes knowledge, that we may be filled with all of the fullness of God (Eph. 3:18-19). God wants you to walk in Love always. To walk in Love is to walk in peace with all men. Renewing your mind in the Word of God will help you to know God and His Character so that you may be transformed by the renewing of your mind, that you may prove what is that good and acceptable and perfect will of God (Rom. 12:2).

When you renew your mind in His Word, you can begin to

practice imitating His ways by the power of the Holy Spirit (Eph. 5:1). Therefore, Jesus shows us how we should love all people, as this is one of His greatest commands.

Chapter Three

Be Strong! Be Brave on your Journey!
"I have told you these things, so that in Me you may have [perfect] peace and confidence. In the world you have tribulation and trials and distress and frustration; but be of good cheer [take courage; be confident, certain, undaunted]! For I have overcome the world. [I have deprived it of power to harm you and have conquered it for you.] John 16:33 Amp.

On your journey with Christ you will experience the warfare of the Believer. This speaks of your encounters with hostile forces that sometimes manifest themselves in people and circumstances. These hostile forces are mentioned in Ephesians 6:10-13 and they are already defeated because of your commitment to walk in love wearing the full armor of God.

When encountering difficult people and/or circumstances, do not be alarmed and do not be afraid as if something strange is happening to you, but be of good cheer because Jesus has overcome the world and everything in it. God has deprived it of power to harm you (1 Peter 4:12-13; John 16:33). You are His chosen vessel of honor!

> *Therefore, count it all joy when you fall into divers trials knowing that the testing of your faith produces patience. But let patience have its perfect work, that you may be perfect and complete, lacking nothing (James 1:2-4).*

The circumstances must bow to the

authority of the Lord. The circumstances will do what Jesus says! I encourage you to say what Jesus says! Speak abundant life, healing, and deliverance. Speak in Jesus Name (2 Cor. 10:4-5).

It is very important to remember that we do not wrestle against flesh and blood, but against principalities, against powers, against the rulers of the darkness of this age, against spiritual hosts of wickedness in the heavenly places (Eph. 6:10-12).

When you encounter a person or circumstance that demonstrates hatred towards you this means that the situation is attempting to injure you because of intense hostility caused by the adversary, the devil. Even in the face of these dangers, your salvation in Jesus Christ prevails and works on your behalf. You have triumphed over every opposition according to God's Word in Isaiah 54:17. No weapon that is formed against you shall prosper; and every tongue that shall rise against you in judgment you shall condemn. This is the heritage of the servants of the Lord, and their righteousness is of me, saith the Lord (Isaiah 54:17).

For example, the Apostle Paul endured many hardships, trials, and persecutions yet God led him and helped him to stand under, endure, and undertake everyone of them. His great example helps us to better understand the sufferings and consolations that we share with our Savior. God is able to protect and defend you and give you a testimony. That is what He has also done for me and He will do the same for you. God is no respecter of persons. What He will do for one, He will do for all. Your testimony derives from the test you endured, stood under, and undertook by the power of God and with the help of the Holy Spirit. With your testimony you will bear witness to the power of the truth of the Gospel of Jesus Christ, just as I did. You will testify and be His witness (John 15:27) ! In my tests and in every circumstance in my life, I remain confident in God's Power and His ability to Perform His Word, to Deliver me and Provide for me daily. This must be your stance of faith also; to fully expect God to move on your behalf and to work all things together for your good. By continuing to have faith, you will endure until the end and save your lives according to Matt. 24:13; for we have around us many people whose lives tell us what faith means, so let us run the race that is before us and never give up (Heb. 12:1).

The Patriarchs such as Abraham,

Isaac, and Jacob and many others such as Gideon, Barak, Samson and David triumphed in life because of their faith (Heb. 11:17-40). We can even look to our Lord Jesus as our example of triumphant faith, who endured hostility from sinners against Him and His suffering when He was nailed to the cross for our sins. So do not become weary and discouraged (Heb. 12:3).

Take a look at Matthew 5:43-48. Jesus tells us in Matthew 5:44 what we should do when faced with the tests and trials that will give us our testimonies. Jesus says we must not only pray for those we love and those who are lovable, but we must also pray for those who hurt us. This is how we love our enemies. To see them living for Jesus and walking upright and victorious before Him must be our desire.

Jesus desires to lead and guide you and make your life fruitful (Ps. 32:8; John 15:5). In living and walking closely with Him you will know that you can always be of good cheer! There is power and victory in Jesus Christ who has overcome the world (John 16:33).

Chapter Four

FOR YOU, YOUR NATION, AND ALL ACCOMPANYING YOU

"Blessed is the nation whose God is the Lord, The people He has chosen as His own inheritance."
Psalm 33:12

It is important to understand that God's salvation brought to you through Jesus is not only personally for you, but it is also for your Nation and all accompanying you! Just as God sent Moses to deliver the people of Israel out of slavery in Egypt, so your Nation will be delivered by the hand of God. So it is by faith that we must believe that our Nation will be delivered, rescued, and saved by God. Luke 1:69-71 tells more about what our personal and National security entails:

> "...*He (God) has raised up a horn of salvation for us...That we should be saved from our enemies, and from the hand of all who hate us....*"

When Paul traveled to Rome in Acts 27: 23-25, a terrible storm arose. Since he belonged to God, Paul and ALL those who sailed with him were saved. God has a purpose for you, your life, and your Nation. By believing on Jesus, you and all who goes with you will be saved. Wherever you go, your salvation benefits goes with you and are a gift from God for your safety and health right now. It is the power in the Love of Jesus that saves! There is no one else who saves like Jesus and there is no other name under heaven given among men by which we must be saved (Acts 4:12).

Believing in Jesus and confessing that He is Lord, grants you your salvation benefits that Jesus died to give you.

> *For with the heart one believes unto righteousness, and with the mouth confession is made unto salvation (Romans 10:10) .*

It is through Christ that we are saved from God's anger, because we have been made right with God by the Blood of His Son Jesus Christ. While we were God's enemies, He made friends with us through the death of His Son (Romans 5:9-11 NCV). God gives good gifts and wants you to have and enjoy everything that He has for you. God does not want you to fall prey to the adversary. Nor does He want you to be led astray and subjected to Satan's senseless influences.

God's word speaks and by faith we must move with godly fear on His word like Noah did when God divinely warned him of the flood. Noah's obedience and faith in God saved him and his household (Gen. 6:13-22; Heb. 11:7). Jesus has come to deliver you, your house, and your Nation.

The Accuser comes to steal, kill and destroy but your Deliverer (Jesus!) has come so that you may have and enjoy life, and have it in abundance (to the full, till it overflows) (John 10:10b AMP).
No devil can hinder the life, liberty, and victory that you have in God's word. Nothing can hinder or destroy the life, liberty, and victory that we all have as Believers in Jesus Christ.   God's word is truth and light in this dark and sinful world. Jesus wants your heart to know the victory in His Blood which speaks of better things for you, your Nation

and your future (Lev. 17:11; Matt. 26:28; Jer. 29:11). If you confess with your mouth that Jesus is Lord and believe in your heart that God raised Him from the dead you will be saved (Rom. 10:9).

Chapter Five

SPIRITUAL AND ETERNAL SALVATION NOW!

"She will bear a Son, and you shall call His name Jesus [the Greek form of the Hebrew Joshua, which means Savior], for He will save His people from their sins [that is, prevent them from failing and missing the true end and scope of life, which is God]." Matt. 1:21 Amp.

Surrendering to Jesus today ensures your spiritual and eternal salvation and it is granted immediately by God to those who believe on the Lord Jesus Christ (Eph. 2:4-8; 1 Tim. 2:4). To be saved means that Jesus has come [into your heart] to help you and deliver you daily (Rom. 5:10 AMP): to remove all burdens and set you free from every bondage in your life. Today you are giving Him every burden in your heart.

    When you invite Jesus into your heart and you believe on Him you join forces with the Creator of Heaven and earth (Love) to forge a single and stronger fighting unit (1 John 4:4; 1 John 4:8; 1 Cor. 12:31; 1 Cor. 13:4-8). Only now God fights all your battles and you are just in agreement with Him and His word by walking in Love (2 John 6; 1 Cor. 13:4-8). In truth, He has already given you the victory against sickness, disease and lack. He has won every battle you will ever face. Jesus says take my yoke upon you and learn from Me for My yoke is easy and My burden is light (Matt. 11:29-30).

It does not mean that you will not encounter trials and persecutions; it does mean that you have conquered every one of them (Rom. 8:37). The Word says in Ps. 34:19 that "Many are the afflictions of the righteous **but the Lord delivers him out of them all**." If you have not already received Jesus as your Lord and Savior, I encourage you to get in agreement with God! Speak God's Word and invite Jesus into your heart today.

PRAYER FOR SALVATION AND BAPTISM IN THE HOLY SPIRIT

Heavenly Father, I come to You today in the name of Jesus. Father forgive me of my sins. I ask Jesus to come into my heart and be Lord over my life (Romans 10:9-10, Romans 5:10, and Acts 2:21). I confess that Jesus is Lord and I believe in my heart that God raised Him from the dead (1 Cor. 15:20-25).

Thank you Lord Jesus! Now I am reborn! I am a Christian - a very victorious child of Almighty God! I am saved!

Father I'm also asking You to fill me with the Holy Spirit. Holy Spirit I receive you and I welcome you into my heart. I fully expect to speak with other tongues as You give me the utterance (Acts 1:8; Acts 2:4; 1Cor. 14:2; Luke 11:13).

Hallelujah! Thank You Jesus!

YOU ARE MORE THAN A CONQUEROR!

HALLELUJAH! Now you can rest assured knowing that God will bring you safely through and you are saved! Continue to thank and praise God for filling you with His Spirit (John 16:13). Speak to the Lord in your new Heavenly language. These are special words and unique syllables given to you by the Holy Spirit (1 Cor. 14:2). You are not going to understand what you're saying, but the Spirit of God does and you're talking only to Him (1 Cor. 14:2). Use the gift of the voice God has given you. Line your will up to His Word and

renew your mind in His Word daily (Rom. 12:2). You are now a Spirit-filled Believer! God has given you His blessings and all that belongs to Him belongs to you according to John 16:14-15.

Welcome to the Family of God!!

ABOUT JESUS

Jesus Christ, full of grace and truth, is the Author of eternal salvation unto all of them that believes in Him. *"...that if you confess with your mouth and believe in your heart that God has raised Jesus from the dead, you will be saved. For with the heart one believes unto righteousness, and with the mouth confession that is made unto salvation. For the Scripture says, 'Whoever believes on Him will not be put to shame.' For there is no distinction between Jew and Greek; for the same Lord over all is rich to all who call upon Him. For 'whoever calls on the name of the Lord shall be saved.' For in Mount Zion and in Jerusalem there shall be deliverance."* (Rom. 10:9-13; Joel 2:32)

He is the real and effectual cause of our salvation. He Himself is our salvation (Luke 2:30; 3:6; Heb. 2:10-11). He was in the beginning with God and He is the Living

Word of God. All things were made through Him and without Him nothing was made that was made (John 1:1-3) We as (Believers in Jesus Christ) are seated with Him now in Heavenly places because of God and His great Love (Eph. 2:4). *"For by grace we have been saved through faith, and not of ourselves; it is the gift of God, not of works, lest anyone should boast. For we are His workmanship, created in Christ Jesus for good works, which God prepared beforehand that we should walk in them. (Eph. 2:8-10)."*

In Him was life, and the life was the light of men. And the light shines in the darkness, and the darkness did not comprehend it. (John 1:4-5) And His Light overpowers darkness. And the Word (Jesus) became flesh and dwelt among us, and we beheld His glory, the glory as of the only begotten of the Father, full of grace and truth. Jesus is a Healer, a

Teacher, a Miracle Worker, Apostle, Great High Priest and Intercessor. He is a Preacher, a Prophet, Prince of Peace, the Lord our Righteousness, Wisdom, Lord, Savior, Treasure and so much more that words cannot even explain He is our God!

ABOUT THE AUTHOR

Ms. Misha G. Benjamin is the Founder and President of The Wordflowers Corporation. Wordflowers is a Christian Publishing Company that speaks and distinctively praises God's Word in the earth. At Wordflowers, Ms. Benjamin is also a Writer and Author who specializes in Christian and Children's Literature. Ms. Benjamin is a graduate of the Institute of Children's Literature. Ms. Benjamin also works as a Volunteer Teacher for English Speakers of Other Languages (ESOL) and also as a Children's Story-Time Reader. Ms. Benjamin currently resides in Woodbridge, VA.

UPCOMING RELEASES BY THE AUTHOR!

- Egypt, Assyria, Israel and their God
- Agape's Performance

WORDFLOWERS

Your questions, inquiries, and requests for more information are welcome at:

info@wordflowerscorp.org

You may also visit our website at: www.wordflowers.org.

NOTES:

NOTES:

NOTES:

NOTES:

NOTES:

NOTES:

NOTES:

NOTES:

NOTES:

NOTES:

NOTES:

NOTES:

www.ingramcontent.com/pod-product-compliance
Lightning Source LLC
Chambersburg PA
CBHW032017290426
44109CB00013B/687